OPERATIONS MASTERY

MANAGING THE FLOW OF VALUE IN BUSINESS

DR. JAGADEESH PILLAI

Made with ♥ on the Notion Press Platform
www.notionpress.com

|| Dedicated to all wisdom seekers around the world ||

Contents

Contents

Prayer

"Om Bhadram Karnebhih Shrunuyaama DevaahBhadram Pashyemaakshabhiryajatraah Sthirairangaistushtuvaamsastanoobhih Vyashema Devahitam YadaayuhSwasti Na Indro VridhashravaahSwasti Nah Pooshaa VishwavedaahSwasti Nastaarkshyo ArishtanemihSwasti No Brihaspatir DadhaatuOm Shantih, Shantih, Shantih"

The literal meaning of this mantra is: OM. O Gods! Let us hear auspicious words from our ears. O reverent Gods! Let us behold propitious visions from our eyes, let our organs and body be stable, healthy, and strong. Let us do that which is pleasing to the gods in the life span allotted to us. May Indra, inscribed in the scriptures, bring us fortune! May Pushan, the knower of the world, grant us prosperity! May Trakshya, who vanquishes enemies, bestow us with blessings! May Brihaspati bring us success!
OM Peace, Peace, Peace.

About The Author

Dr. Jagadeesh Pillai is a renowned Guinness World Record holder, writer, and researcher hailing from Varanasi, also known as the abode of Lord Shiva. With a Ph.D. in Vedic Science and a range of creative ideas and achievements, he is a true polymath. He is the author of more than 100 books including Research Publications. Although his roots can be traced back to Kerala, the people of Varanasi hold him in high regard and affectionately consider him one of their own.

In 1998, Dr. Pillai was offered a job at Banaras Hindu University, but he left the position after only two months to pursue greater goals in life. He believed that in order to study Indian scriptures and engage in other creative endeavours, he needed to retire from the daily grind of working solely for money at a young age.

He started an export business from scratch, using the knowledge he had gained from a previous job in the industry. His intelligence and unique approach to business led to great success in a short period of time, earning him more in just a decade and a half than he would have in a lifetime working in a government job. Upon the passing of Dr. APJ Abdul Kalam, Dr. Pillai decided to leave the business and dedicate himself to reading, studying, researching, and experimenting.

During his tenure in the export business, Dr. Pillai traveled to over 16 countries, gaining valuable insight and experiencing the world and life in detail.

Dr. Pillai has achieved four Guinness World Records in the following subjects:

"Script to Screen" - In this record, Dr. Pillai produced and directed an animation film within the shortest time possible, breaking the previous record set by Canadians. He has also received numerous national and international awards and recognitions for this achievement.

Longest Line of Postcards - For this record, Dr. Pillai created a line of 16,300 postcards on the occasion of the 163rd anniversary of Indian Postal Day. The event also included a questionnaire about the Indian flag.

Largest Poster Awareness Campaign - Dr. Pillai designed an awareness campaign on the subject of "Beti Bachao - Beti Padhao" (Save the Girl Child - Educate the Girl Child) to achieve this record.

Largest Envelope - In tribute to the Indian Prime Minister's "Make in India" initiative, Dr. Pillai created a 4000 square meter envelope using waste paper to achieve this record.

Attempted - **70000 Candles on a 210 kg Cake** - To celebrate the 70th Indian Independence Day, Dr. Pillai attempted to light 70,000 candles on a 210 kg cake, which was recorded in World Records India.

Attempted - **Documentary on Dhamek Stupa of Sarnath in 17 Languages** - Dr. Pillai attempted to create a documentary on the Dhamek Stupa of Sarnath, dubbing it in 17 different languages. The result of this attempt is currently awaiting confirmation from the Guinness World Records.

Dr. Pillai is skilled in teaching the Bhagavad Gita, a Hindu scripture, and is popular among young people. He has helped many young people improve their lives through his motivational teachings.

In addition to teaching, he has composed and sung numerous Sanskrit Bhajans and patriotic songs.

He has also written and directed several short films and documentaries for awareness campaigns, and has volunteered with the police in both UP and Kerala to spread awareness about various issues through videos and photography.

Incredibly, he has produced and directed over 100 documentaries about the city of Varanasi, all on his own.

He has also helped and guided more than 25 boys and girls to achieve world records through creative and innovative methods. He is a multifaceted person who uses his intellect and the blessings given to him by God to excel in various areas. He is both a teacher and a student, always learning and teaching, and is able to master any subject he comes across.

He is a selfless social activist and motivational speaker who has overcome struggles and failures to become a successful and enthusiastic individual with a rich life experience.

In addition to his work with the Bhagavad Gita, he is also an efficient Tarot card reader, Astro-Vastu consultant, and a talented singer and composer. He has sung the entire Ram Charita Manas and Bhagavad Gita in his own compositions, and has sung the phrase "Lokah Samastha Sukhino Bhavantu" in 50 different languages. He is currently working on a detailed and scientific study of Vedas, Upanishads, Puranas, and the Bhagavad Gita. He has also composed and sung the Hanuman Chalisa and Gayatri Mantra in 108 and 1008 different compositions, respectively.

Awards - Four Times Guinness World Records, Winner of Mahatma Gandhi Vishwa Shanti Puraskar, Mahatma Gandhi Global Peace Ambassador, Kashi Ratna Award, Dr. APJ Abdul Kalam Motivational Person of the Year 2017, Mother Teresa Award, Indira Gandhi Priyadarshini Award, Bharat Vikas Ratna Award, Udyog Ratna Award, Vigyan Prasar Award, Poorvanchal Ratn Samman.

Preface

It is with great pleasure that I introduce the new book, "Operations Mastery: Managing the Flow of Value in Business." This book is a comprehensive guide to mastering the operations of any business, from small startups to large corporations. It provides readers with the knowledge and tools to effectively manage the flow of value in their business, from the production of goods and services to the delivery of customer satisfaction.

This book is an invaluable resource for anyone looking to gain a better understanding of the operations of their business. It covers topics such as process optimization, resource allocation, and customer service, as well as providing practical advice on how to implement these strategies. It also provides a comprehensive overview of the latest trends in operations management, including the use of technology and automation.

The book is written in an easy-to-understand style, making it accessible to readers of all levels of experience. It is packed with real-world examples and case studies, making it an invaluable resource for anyone looking to improve their operations.

This book is a must-have for anyone looking to gain a better understanding of the operations of their business. It is an essential guide for anyone looking to maximize the flow of value in their business and ensure customer satisfaction. With its comprehensive coverage of operations management, this book is sure to become an invaluable resource for anyone looking to take their business to the next level.

ONE

Introduction to Operations Management

Operations management is the practice of managing the operations of a business or organization in order to maximize efficiency and achieve its stated objectives. It requires an understanding of the principles of operations and the ability to apply those principles to the strategic, tactical, and operational decisions of a business. This chapter provides an overview of operations management, including its history, key concepts, and common practices.

Origins of Operations Management

Operations management has its roots in the industrial revolution of the 19th century, when factories and production lines began to be used to mass-produce items. Since that time, the principles of operations management have been refined and evolved to meet the needs of modern businesses. In the 1950s and 1960s, operations management emerged as an academic discipline, and today, it is a well-established field of study.

What is Operations Management?

Operations management is the practice of balancing cost, quality, and speed in order to optimize the production of goods or services. It involves identifying and implementing policies, procedures, and processes to ensure the efficient use of resources and the achievement of organizational goals. It can also refer to the management of the supply chain, which includes the movement of raw materials and finished goods from suppliers to customers.

Key Concepts in Operations Management

The key concepts in operations management include service design, process design, operations planning, forecasting, capacity planning, supply chain management, inventory control, and quality management. These concepts are used to improve the efficiency and effectiveness of production processes and to minimize costs. Each of these concepts is discussed in more detail in the following sections.

Service Design

Service design is the process of designing services to meet customer needs. It involves analyzing customer preferences and determining which aspects of the service to emphasize, as well as how to deliver the service. It requires the identification of key components, such as the delivery system, quality, and cost.

Process Design

Process design is the process of designing the production process to reduce costs and improve quality. It requires the development of an effective production process that is efficient and cost-effective. The process includes the identification of resources, the selection of equipment, and the development of a layout that ensures the efficient use of space and equipment.

Operations Planning

Operations planning is the process of creating a comprehensive plan for the effective and efficient utilization of resources. It involves analyzing current operations, identifying areas of improvement, and developing strategies to optimize performance. This process requires careful consideration of the organization's goals, objectives, and resources, as well as an understanding of the external environment. By taking a proactive approach to operations planning, organizations can ensure that their operations are running smoothly and efficiently, while also positioning themselves for future success.

TWO

Operations Strategy

Operations strategy is a long-term approach to managing organizational resources for the purpose of achieving organizational objectives. It involves the identification of goals and objectives and the development of plans and policies to achieve them. It is based on the principles of operations management and focuses on the four core components of operations: people, processes, technology, and the environment. This chapter will discuss the key elements of operations strategy and the importance of aligning operations strategy with the organization's overall strategy.

Elements of Operations Strategy

The key elements of operations strategy include service design, process design, capacity planning, supply chain management, inventory control, quality management, and performance measurement. Each of these elements is discussed in more detail in the following sections.

Service Design

Service design is the process of designing services to meet customer needs. It involves analyzing customer preferences and determining which aspects of the service to emphasize, as well as how to deliver the service. It requires the identification of key components, such as the delivery system, quality, and cost.

Process Design

Process design is the process of designing the production process to reduce costs and improve quality. It requires the development of an effective production process that is efficient and cost-effective. The process includes the identification of resources, the selection of equipment, and the development of a layout that ensures the efficient use of space and equipment.

Capacity Planning

Capacity planning is the process of determining the capacity of the organization to produce goods or services. It involves determining the number and type of resources needed to meet the organizational objectives. Capacity planning also involves designing the production process, determining the level of automation, and selecting the appropriate technology and equipment.

Supply Chain Management

Supply chain management is the practice of managing the

supply chain to create value for the organization and its customers. It involves identifying suppliers, negotiating contracts, monitoring supplier performance, and managing inventory. It also involves coordinating with other organizations in the supply chain to ensure timely delivery of goods.

Inventory Control

Inventory control is a critical process for any organization, as it ensures that customer needs are met while also providing an accurate picture of inventory levels. It involves monitoring inventory levels, tracking inventory flows, and forecasting demand to ensure that the organization is well-stocked and prepared for customer orders. By utilizing inventory control, organizations can maximize efficiency and minimize costs, allowing them to remain competitive in the marketplace.

THREE

Process Analysis and Design

Process Analysis and Design is a powerful tool for organizations to optimize their operations and achieve their objectives. It involves a comprehensive understanding of the current process, its strengths and weaknesses, and its potential for improvement. This chapter provides an overview of the key concepts and techniques of process analysis and design, as well as the potential benefits it can bring.

The Benefits of Process Analysis and Design

Process analysis and design can bring a range of advantages to organizations, such as increased efficiency, cost savings, improved customer satisfaction, and improved product quality. By analyzing existing processes and identifying areas for improvement, organizations can better meet their customer and business needs.

Key Concepts of Process Analysis and Design

The key concepts of process analysis and design include process mapping, process improvement, process optimization, and process automation. Process mapping involves creating a visual representation of the current process, which can help identify areas for improvement. Process improvement involves making changes to the process to increase efficiency and reduce costs. Process optimization involves finding the most efficient way to complete a process. Finally, process automation involves using technology to automate certain tasks, which can reduce the amount of manual labor required.

FOUR

Capacity Planning

Capacity planning is the process of determining the facilities, personnel, and resources required to meet the demand for a particular product or service. It is a crucial part of operations management, as it allows businesses to maximize their output while minimizing its costs. In order for capacity planning to be successful, organizations must have an accurate forecast of their demand, as well as an understanding of the resources required to meet that demand.

Overview of Capacity Planning

Capacity planning is a process used to identify and analyze the resources required to meet the demand for a product or service. It consists of three main steps: forecasting, resource analysis, and capacity optimization.

Forecasting involves estimating future demand and determining the resources that will be needed to meet that demand. Resource analysis involves determining the amount of resources needed to meet the forecasted demand. And capacity optimization involves determining the most efficient way to allocate the resources to meet the demand.

Benefits of Capacity Planning

There are a number of benefits to having an effective capacity planning system in place. It allows organizations to maximize their production efficiency and minimize their costs. It also allows them to plan for future growth and respond to changes in demand. Additionally, it can help organizations avoid overloading their resources and help them identify potential issues before they become problems.

Capacity Planning Framework

A capacity planning framework is a set of components designed to help organizations plan for their capacity needs. It typically consists of a number of components, including demand forecasting, resource analysis, capacity optimization, and performance metrics. Each component is designed to help the organization identify and analyze the resources required to meet the demand for their product or service.

Challenges of Capacity Planning

Although capacity planning can be a powerful tool, there are several challenges organizations must face when they are implementing a capacity planning system. These include properly estimating demand, understanding the resources required to meet demand, and optimizing capacity in a way that minimizes costs. Additionally, organizations must be able to respond to changes in demand and make necessary adjustments to their capacity plan.

Conclusion

Capacity planning is a crucial component of operations management. It involves forecasting, resource analysis, and capacity optimization, and it can help organizations maximize their efficiency and minimize their costs. However, it is not without its challenges, and organizations must be prepared to respond to changes in demand and make necessary adjustments to their capacity plan.

FIVE

SCHEDULING

Scheduling is the process of organizing and coordinating activities within an organization. It involves determining the timing and sequence of tasks, assigning resources to them, and monitoring progress. Scheduling is essential for ensuring that tasks are completed on time and within budget. It is an important part of operations management and can help organizations achieve their goals in the most efficient and cost-effective way possible.

Overview of Scheduling

Scheduling is a process used to identify and organize tasks and resources in order to complete a project or achieve a goal. It determines the timing and sequence of tasks, assigns resources to them, and monitors progress. It is an integral part of operations management and can help organizations maximize their efficiency and minimize their costs.

Benefits of Scheduling

Scheduling can help organizations achieve their goals in the most efficient and cost-effective way possible. It can improve project completion times, reduce risks associated with resource constraints, and increase efficiency. Additionally, it can help organizations plan for the future and respond to changes in demand.

Scheduling Framework

A scheduling framework is a set of components designed to help organizations plan and manage their activities. It typically consists of a number of components, including task sequencing, resource allocation, tracking, and reporting. Each component is designed to help the organization identify and organize tasks and resources in order to complete a project or achieve a goal.

Challenges of Scheduling

Although scheduling can be a powerful tool, there are several challenges organizations must face when they are implementing a scheduling system. These include properly estimating demand, understanding the resources required to meet demand, and optimizing scheduling in a way that minimizes costs. Additionally, organizations must be able to respond to changes in demand and make necessary adjustments to their schedule.

Conclusion

Scheduling is an important part of operations management. It involves task sequencing, resource allocation, tracking, and reporting and can help organizations achieve their goals in the most efficient and cost-effective way possible. However, it is not without its challenges, and organizations must be prepared to respond to changes in demand and make necessary adjustments to their schedule.

SIX

Inventory Management

Inventory management is the process of tracking and managing a company's inventory. It involves tracking and monitoring inventory levels, forecasting demand, and determining the optimal level of inventory to have on hand. It is an important part of operations management, as it helps organizations maximize their efficiency and minimize their costs.

Overview of Inventory Management

Inventory management is a process used to identify, track, and manage a company's inventory. It involves tracking and monitoring inventory levels, forecasting demand, and determining the optimal level of inventory to have on hand. It is an essential part of operations management and can help organizations maximize their production efficiency and minimize their costs.

Benefits of Inventory Management

There are a number of benefits to having an effective inventory management system in place. It allows organizations to reduce their costs by ensuring they have the right amount of inventory on hand. It also helps them to reduce the risk of stock outs, which can have a negative impact on customer satisfaction. Additionally, it can help organizations increase their profits by reducing the amount of money tied up in inventory.

Inventory Management Framework

An inventory management framework is a set of components designed to help organizations plan for their inventory needs. It typically consists of a number of components, including demand forecasting, inventory tracking, optimization, and reporting. Each component is designed to help the organization identify, track, and manage their inventory in a way that maximizes efficiency and minimizes costs.

Challenges of Inventory Management

Although inventory management can be a powerful tool, there are several challenges organizations must face when they are implementing an inventory management system. These include properly estimating demand, understanding the resources required to meet demand, and optimizing inventory in a way that minimizes costs. Additionally, organizations must be able to respond to changes in demand and make necessary adjustments to their inventory plan.

Conclusion

Inventory management is an important part of operations management. It involves tracking and monitoring inventory levels, forecasting demand, and determining the optimal level of inventory to have on hand in order to meet customer demand while minimizing costs. It also includes managing the flow of inventory, including purchasing, receiving, storing, and shipping. Effective inventory management helps organizations to reduce costs, improve customer service, and increase efficiency.

SEVEN

QUALITY MANAGEMENT

Quality management is the process of ensuring that products and services meet or exceed customer expectations. It involves setting quality standards, measuring performance, and then taking corrective action to ensure that these standards are met. Quality management is a vital part of operations management and can help organizations maximize their efficiency and minimize their costs.

Overview of Quality Management

Quality management is the process of ensuring that products and services meet or exceed customer expectations. It involves setting quality standards, measuring performance, and then taking corrective action to ensure that these standards are met. It is an important part of operations management and can help organizations achieve their goals in the most efficient and cost-effective way possible.

Benefits of Quality Management

There are a number of benefits to having an effective quality management system in place. It allows organizations to maximize their production efficiency and minimize their costs. It also allows them to plan for future growth and respond to changes in demand. Additionally, it can help organizations avoid costly defects and improve customer satisfaction.

Quality Management Framework

A quality management framework is a set of components designed to help organizations meet their quality objectives. It typically consists of a number of components, including setting quality standards, measuring performance, and taking corrective actions. Each component is designed to help the organization identify and analyze the resources required to meet their quality objectives

Challenges of Quality Management

Although quality management can be a powerful tool, there are several challenges organizations must face when they are implementing a quality management system. These include setting appropriate quality standards, measuring performance, and taking corrective action when necessary. Additionally, organizations must be able to respond to changes in demand and make necessary adjustments to their quality plan.

Conclusion

Quality management is an important component of operations management. It involves setting quality standards, measuring performance, and taking corrective action, and it can help organizations maximize their efficiency and minimize their costs. However, it is not without its challenges, and organizations must be prepared to respond to changes in demand and make necessary adjustments to their quality plan.

EIGHT

LEAN AND SIX SIGMA

Lean and Six Sigma are two quality management methodologies used to improve the efficiency and effectiveness of operations. Lean is a process improvement methodology that focuses on eliminating waste and streamlining processes. Six Sigma is a data-driven approach to quality improvement that focuses on reducing variation and improving process performance. Both Lean and Six Sigma are used to help organizations improve their production efficiency and minimize their costs.

Overview of Lean and Six Sigma

Lean and Six Sigma are two quality management methodologies used to improve the efficiency and effectiveness of operations. Lean is a process improvement methodology that focuses on eliminating waste and streamlining processes. Six Sigma is a data-driven approach to quality improvement that focuses on reducing variation and improving process performance. Both Lean and Six

Sigma are used to help organizations achieve their goals in the most efficient and cost-effective way possible.

Benefits of Lean and Six Sigma

There are a number of benefits to implementing Lean and Six Sigma methodologies. It allows organizations to maximize their production efficiency and minimize their costs. It also helps them to reduce the risk of errors, which can have a negative impact on customer satisfaction. Additionally, it can help organizations increase their profits by reducing the amount of money tied up in inventory.

Lean and Six Sigma Framework

A Lean and Six Sigma framework is a set of components designed to help organizations improve their operations. It typically consists of a number of components, including process mapping, process improvement, and performance measurement. Each component is designed to help the organization identify and analyze the resources required to meet their goals.

Challenges of Lean and Six Sigma

Although Lean and Six Sigma can be powerful tools, there are several challenges organizations must face when they are implementing these methodologies. These include properly understanding the resources required to meet their goals, properly measuring performance, and ensuring the sustainability of the improvement efforts. Additionally, organizations must be able to respond to changes in demand and make necessary adjustments to their plan.

Conclusion

Lean and Six Sigma are two quality management methodologies used to improve the efficiency and effectiveness of operations. They can help organizations maximize their production efficiency and minimize their costs. However, they are not without their challenges, and organizations must be prepared to respond to changes in demand and make necessary adjustments to their plan.

NINE

PROJECT MANAGEMENT

Project management is a critical component of successful business operations. It involves the planning, organizing, and controlling of resources to achieve specific goals. It is a complex process that requires a deep understanding of the organization's objectives, resources, and constraints.

Project management is a key factor in the success of any business. It helps to ensure that projects are completed on time, within budget, and to the highest quality standards. It also helps to ensure that projects are aligned with the organization's overall goals and objectives.

Project management involves a variety of activities, including planning, scheduling, resource allocation, risk management, and communication. It requires a comprehensive understanding of the project's scope, objectives, and timeline. It also requires the ability to identify and manage risks, as well as the ability to effectively communicate with stakeholders.

Project management is a complex process that requires a great deal of skill and experience. It requires the ability to think strategically, to plan and organize resources, and to manage risks. It also requires the ability to effectively communicate with stakeholders and to motivate team members.

Project management is an essential part of successful business operations. It helps to ensure that projects are completed on time, within budget, and to the highest quality standards. It also helps to ensure that projects are aligned with the organization's overall goals and objectives. By leveraging the right project management tools and techniques, organizations can ensure that their projects are successful and that their operations are running smoothly.

TEN

Supply Chain Management

Supply chain management is a critical component of operations mastery. It involves the coordination of activities across the entire supply chain, from the procurement of raw materials to the delivery of finished products to customers. By managing the flow of materials, information, and money, supply chain management helps organizations maximize efficiency and minimize costs.

At its core, supply chain management is about creating value. It involves the strategic planning and execution of activities that enable organizations to deliver products and services to customers in a timely and cost-effective manner. This includes the selection of suppliers, the optimization of inventory levels, and the coordination of transportation and logistics.

In addition to creating value, supply chain management also helps organizations reduce risk. By managing the flow of materials, information, and money, organizations can better anticipate and respond to changes in the market. This helps them reduce the risk of supply chain disruptions, which can have a significant impact on their bottom line.

Finally, supply chain management helps organizations build relationships with their suppliers and customers. By understanding their needs and working together to meet them, organizations can create long-term partnerships that benefit both parties. This helps organizations build trust and loyalty, which can lead to increased sales and profits.

In short, supply chain management is an essential component of operations mastery. By managing the flow of materials, information, and money, organizations can create value, reduce risk, and build relationships with their suppliers and customers. By doing so, they can ensure that their operations are running smoothly and efficiently, and that their customers are receiving the best possible service.

ELEVEN

Logistics and Distribution

Logistics and distribution are essential components of any successful business operation. They are responsible for ensuring that goods and services are delivered to customers in a timely and cost-effective manner. Logistics and distribution involve the coordination of resources, such as transportation, inventory, and personnel, to ensure that goods and services are delivered to the right place, at the right time, and in the right condition.

The logistics and distribution process begins with the selection of a suitable transportation method. This could include air, land, or sea freight, depending on the size and weight of the goods being shipped. Once the transportation method is chosen, the goods must be packaged and labeled correctly to ensure that they arrive safely and on time.

Next, the goods must be stored in an appropriate warehouse or distribution center. This is where inventory management comes into play. Inventory management involves tracking the quantity and quality of goods in the warehouse, as well as ensuring that the right goods are shipped to the right customers.

Finally, the goods must be delivered to the customer. This is where distribution comes into play. Distribution involves the coordination of resources, such as personnel, vehicles, and routes, to ensure that goods are delivered to the customer in a timely and cost-effective manner.

Logistics and distribution are essential components of any successful business operation. They are responsible for ensuring that goods and services are delivered to customers in a timely and cost-effective manner. By carefully managing the flow of goods and services, businesses can maximize their profits and ensure customer satisfaction. With the right logistics and distribution strategy, businesses can ensure that their operations run smoothly and efficiently.

TWELVE

MANUFACTURING AND ASSEMBLY

Manufacturing and assembly are two of the most important components of operations management. They are the processes that turn raw materials into finished products, and they are essential for any business to be successful.

Manufacturing is the process of transforming raw materials into finished products. It involves a variety of activities, such as cutting, shaping, and assembling components. It also involves the use of machines and tools to create the desired product. The goal of manufacturing is to create a product that meets the customer's needs and specifications.

Assembly is the process of putting together the components of a product. It involves the use of machines, tools, and manual labor to assemble the components into a finished product. Assembly is a critical step in the manufacturing process, as it ensures that the product is of the highest quality and meets the customer's expectations.

Both manufacturing and assembly are essential for any business to be successful. They are the processes that turn raw materials into finished products, and they are essential for any business to be successful. Manufacturing and assembly processes must be carefully planned and managed in order to ensure that the product meets the customer's needs and specifications.

Manufacturing and assembly are complex processes that require a great deal of skill and expertise. It is important for businesses to have a team of experienced professionals who understand the intricacies of these processes and can ensure that the product is of the highest quality.

In conclusion, manufacturing and assembly are two of the most important components of operations management. They are the processes that turn raw materials into finished products, and they are essential for any business to be successful. It is important for businesses to have a team of experienced professionals who understand the intricacies of these processes and can ensure that the product is of the highest quality. With the right team in place, businesses can ensure that their products meet the customer's needs and specifications, and that they are able to remain competitive in the market.

THIRTEEN
SERVICE OPERATIONS

The key to successful service operations is to ensure that the service is delivered in a timely and efficient manner. This requires careful planning and execution of processes and procedures. It also requires the ability to anticipate customer needs and respond quickly to any changes in the environment.

The goal of service operations is to provide a high-quality service that meets customer expectations. This requires a deep understanding of customer needs and the ability to develop and implement strategies to meet those needs. It also requires the ability to monitor and measure the performance of the service and make adjustments as needed.

In order to effectively manage service operations, it is important to have a clear understanding of the customer's needs and expectations. This includes understanding the customer's desired outcomes and the resources available to meet those outcomes. It also requires the ability to develop and implement strategies to meet those needs.

In addition, service operations require the ability to monitor and measure the performance of the service and make adjustments as needed. This includes the ability to identify areas of improvement and develop strategies to address those areas. It also requires the ability to track customer feedback and use it to improve the service.

Finally, service operations require the ability to manage the resources necessary to deliver the service. This includes the ability to allocate resources efficiently and effectively. It also requires the ability to manage the costs associated with the service and ensure that the service is delivered in a cost-effective manner.

By understanding the concept of service operations and how it can be used to manage the flow of value in business, organizations can ensure that they are providing a high-quality service that meets customer expectations. This requires careful planning and execution of processes and procedures, the use of metrics and data analysis to track performance, and continuous improvement efforts to identify and address areas for improvement. Service operations also involve managing resources such as personnel, technology, and equipment, as well as maintaining a strong focus on customer satisfaction and service quality. By effectively managing service operations, organizations can increase customer loyalty, improve their reputation, and ultimately drive revenue growth.

FOURTEEN

TECHNOLOGY AND OPERATIONS

In today's world, technology and operations are inextricably linked. Technology has revolutionized the way businesses operate, allowing them to streamline processes, increase efficiency, and reduce costs. From automation to artificial intelligence, technology has enabled businesses to become more agile and responsive to customer needs.

At the same time, operations have become increasingly complex. Businesses must now manage a wide range of activities, from supply chain management to customer service. To stay competitive, they must be able to quickly adapt to changing market conditions and customer demands.

Technology and operations are two sides of the same coin. Technology enables businesses to become more efficient and responsive, while operations provide the framework for managing the flow of value. By leveraging the power of technology, businesses can optimize their operations and create a competitive advantage.

Technology and operations are also closely intertwined. Technology can be used to automate processes, reduce costs, and improve customer service. At the same time, operations can be used to ensure that technology is used effectively and efficiently. By combining the two, businesses can create a powerful synergy that can help them stay ahead of the competition.

Technology and operations are essential components of any successful business. By leveraging the power of technology and optimizing operations, businesses can create a competitive advantage and maximize their profits. By understanding the relationship between technology and operations, businesses can ensure that they are taking full advantage of the opportunities available to them.

FIFTEEN

ENVIRONMENTAL AND SUSTAINABILITY MANAGEMENT

Environmental and sustainability management is an essential component of successful operations management. It involves the implementation of strategies and practices that reduce the environmental impact of a business while also ensuring that the organization is able to meet its long-term sustainability goals. By taking a proactive approach to environmental and sustainability management, businesses can ensure that their operations are both efficient and sustainable.

The first step in environmental and sustainability management is to identify the environmental impacts of a business's operations. This includes assessing the energy and water usage, waste production, and emissions of the organization. Once these impacts have been identified, the organization can then develop strategies to reduce or eliminate them. This may include implementing energy-efficient technologies, reducing water usage, and improving waste management practices.

The next step is to develop a sustainability plan. This plan should outline the organization's goals for reducing its environmental impact and achieving its sustainability objectives. It should also include strategies for monitoring and measuring progress towards these goals. This plan should be regularly reviewed and updated to ensure that the organization is meeting its sustainability goals.

Finally, the organization should develop a system for reporting on its environmental and sustainability performance. This system should include metrics for measuring progress towards sustainability goals, as well as reporting on the organization's environmental performance. This system should be regularly reviewed and updated to ensure that the organization is meeting its sustainability objectives.

Environmental and sustainability management is an essential component of successful operations management. By taking a proactive approach to environmental and sustainability management, businesses can ensure that their operations are both efficient and sustainable. By identifying the environmental impacts of their operations, developing a sustainability plan, and implementing a system for reporting on their environmental and sustainability performance, businesses can ensure that their operations are both efficient and sustainable.

SIXTEEN

OPERATIONS RESEARCH

Operations Research is a powerful tool for businesses to optimize their operations and maximize their value. It is a field of study that focuses on the development of mathematical models and techniques to analyze and solve complex business problems. By using Operations Research, businesses can identify and address inefficiencies in their operations, improve decision-making, and reduce costs.

Operations Research is a multi-disciplinary field that combines elements of mathematics, statistics, computer science, and engineering. It is used to analyze and optimize complex systems, such as supply chains, transportation networks, and production systems. It can also be used to analyze and improve customer service, marketing, and financial operations.

The goal of Operations Research is to identify the best possible solution to a given problem. This is done by using mathematical models and algorithms to analyze data and identify the most efficient and cost-effective solution. The models and algorithms used in Operations Research are designed to identify the optimal solution to a given problem, taking into account all of the relevant factors.

Operations Research is an invaluable tool for businesses to optimize their operations and maximize their value. By using Operations Research, businesses can identify and address inefficiencies in their operations, improve decision-making, and reduce costs. With the right tools and techniques, businesses can use Operations Research to gain a competitive edge and increase their profitability.

SEVENTEEN

Decision Making

Decision making is a critical component of successful operations management. It is the process of evaluating available options and selecting the best course of action to achieve desired outcomes. The ability to make sound decisions is essential for any business to remain competitive and successful.

When making decisions, it is important to consider the potential risks and rewards associated with each option. This requires a thorough analysis of the situation and a clear understanding of the objectives. It is also important to consider the impact of the decision on stakeholders, such as customers, employees, and shareholders.

The decision-making process should involve gathering and analyzing data, considering alternative solutions, and weighing the pros and cons of each option. It is also important to consider the potential long-term implications of the decision. Once a decision has been made, it is important to monitor the results and adjust the course of action if necessary.

Effective decision making requires a combination of knowledge, experience, and intuition. It is important to be aware of the potential biases that can influence decision making, such as confirmation bias and groupthink. It is also important to be open to new ideas and perspectives.

In conclusion, decision making is a critical component of successful operations management. It requires a combination of knowledge, experience, and intuition, as well as an understanding of potential risks and rewards. By following a structured decision-making process and considering the potential long-term implications of the decision, businesses can ensure that they make the best possible decisions for their operations.

EIGHTEEN

HUMAN RESOURCES AND OPERATIONS

Human Resources (HR) and Operations are two of the most important departments in any business. HR is responsible for managing the people side of the business, while Operations is responsible for managing the processes and systems that enable the business to run smoothly. When these two departments work together, they can create a powerful synergy that drives the success of the business.

HR and Operations have a symbiotic relationship. HR provides the people and the skills needed to run the business, while Operations provides the processes and systems that enable the business to run efficiently. HR and Operations must work together to ensure that the right people are in the right roles, and that the processes and systems are optimized for maximum efficiency.

The key to successful HR and Operations collaboration is communication. HR and Operations must be in constant communication to ensure that the right people are in the right roles, and that the processes and systems are optimized for maximum efficiency. HR and Operations must also be in constant communication to ensure that the business is meeting its goals and objectives.

The goal of Operations Mastery is to create a culture of collaboration between HR and Operations. This means that HR and Operations must work together to ensure that the right people are in the right roles, and that the processes and systems are optimized for maximum efficiency. It also means that HR and Operations must be in constant communication to ensure that the business is meeting its goals and objectives.

By creating a culture of collaboration between HR and Operations, businesses can maximize their potential and achieve their goals. By leveraging the strengths of both departments, businesses can create a powerful synergy that drives the success of the business. By working together, HR and Operations can create a powerful force that will help the business reach its goals and objectives.

NINETEEN
GLOBAL OPERATIONS

In today's globalized world, operations management is essential for businesses to remain competitive. Global operations involve managing the flow of value across multiple countries, cultures, and languages. It requires a deep understanding of the complexities of international markets, as well as the ability to adapt to changing conditions.

Global operations involve a variety of activities, from managing supply chains to developing strategies for international expansion. Companies must be able to identify and capitalize on opportunities in different markets, while also managing risks associated with operating in multiple countries. This requires a comprehensive understanding of the global economy, as well as the ability to develop and implement strategies that are tailored to each market.

In addition to managing the flow of value across multiple

countries, global operations also involve managing the flow of information. Companies must be able to effectively communicate with customers, suppliers, and other stakeholders in different countries. This requires an understanding of different cultures and languages, as well as the ability to develop effective communication strategies.

Finally, global operations involve managing the flow of resources. Companies must be able to identify and access the resources they need to operate in different countries. This includes both physical resources, such as raw materials, and intangible resources, such as intellectual property. Companies must also be able to manage the costs associated with operating in multiple countries, as well as the risks associated with operating in different markets.

Global operations are complex and require a deep understanding of the global economy and the ability to develop and implement strategies tailored to each market. Companies must be able to identify and capitalize on opportunities in different markets, while also managing the flow of value, information, and resources across multiple countries. By mastering the complexities of global operations, businesses can remain competitive in today's globalized world.

TWENTY

Operations and Information Technology

Operations and Information Technology are two of the most important components of any successful business. When it comes to managing the flow of value in business, operations and information technology are essential for ensuring that the business is running smoothly and efficiently.

Operations are the processes and activities that are necessary for the production of goods and services. This includes the planning, organizing, staffing, directing, and controlling of resources to achieve the desired results. Information technology, on the other hand, is the use of computers and software to store, retrieve, and manipulate data. It is used to automate processes, improve communication, and increase efficiency.

When it comes to operations and information technology, it is important to understand how they work together. Operations provide the framework for the business, while information technology provides the tools to make it happen. By combining the two, businesses can create a powerful system that can help them achieve their goals.

In order to maximize the effectiveness of operations and information technology, businesses must have a clear understanding of their goals and objectives. They must also have a plan for how they will use the technology to achieve those goals. Additionally, businesses must have a strategy for how they will use the technology to improve their operations.

Finally, businesses must have a system in place to monitor and evaluate the performance of their operations and information technology. This will help them identify areas of improvement and make necessary changes to ensure that their operations and information technology are working together to create the most value for the business.

By understanding the importance of operations and information technology, businesses can create a powerful system that will help them achieve their goals and maximize the flow of value in their business. By combining operations and information technology, businesses can create a powerful system that will help them achieve their goals and maximize the flow of value in their business. With the right strategy and monitoring system in place, businesses can ensure that their operations and information technology are working together to create the most value for their business and customers. This can include using technology to automate and streamline processes, improve data analysis and decision-making, and enhance communication and collaboration within the organization. By effectively integrating operations and information technology, businesses can improve efficiency, reduce costs, and gain a competitive advantage in their industry. Additionally, by staying up to date with the latest technology trends, businesses can continue to innovate and adapt to changing customer needs and market conditions.

TWENTY-ONE

OPERATIONS IN HEALTHCARE

Operations in healthcare are essential for providing quality care to patients. From the moment a patient enters the hospital, operations are in motion to ensure that they receive the best possible care. From the front desk to the operating room, operations are the backbone of the healthcare system.

Operations in healthcare involve a variety of processes, from scheduling appointments to managing patient records. Every step of the process must be carefully managed to ensure that patients receive the best care possible. In addition, operations must be efficient and cost-effective to ensure that the healthcare system is sustainable.

Operations in healthcare also involve managing the flow of information. This includes collecting and analyzing data to identify trends and areas for improvement. It also involves using technology to streamline processes and improve patient care.

Finally, operations in healthcare involve managing the supply chain. This includes ensuring that the right supplies are available when needed and that they are delivered in a timely manner. It also involves managing inventory levels to ensure that the right supplies are available when needed.

Operations in healthcare are essential for providing quality care to patients. By managing the flow of value in the healthcare system, operations can help ensure that patients receive the best care possible. By using data and technology to streamline processes and improve patient care, operations can help make the healthcare system more efficient and cost-effective. Finally, by managing the supply chain, operations can help ensure that the right supplies are available when needed. By mastering operations in healthcare, healthcare providers can ensure that patients receive the best care possible.

TWENTY-TWO

Operations in Retail

Operations in retail are essential for businesses to succeed. From stocking shelves to managing customer service, operations are the backbone of any retail business. In order to maximize efficiency and profitability, it is important to understand the fundamentals of retail operations.

The first step in managing retail operations is to create a plan. This plan should include a detailed description of the operations, including the roles and responsibilities of each team member. It should also include a timeline for completion of tasks and a budget for any necessary resources.

Once the plan is in place, it is important to ensure that all team members are properly trained and equipped to carry out their duties. This includes providing adequate training on customer service, inventory management, and other operational tasks. Additionally, it is important to ensure that all team members are aware of the company's policies and procedures.

In addition to training, it is important to have a system in place to monitor and measure the performance of the operations. This includes tracking customer satisfaction, inventory levels, and other key performance indicators. By monitoring these metrics, businesses can identify areas of improvement and make necessary changes to ensure that operations are running smoothly.

Finally, it is important to stay up to date on the latest trends in retail operations. This includes staying informed on new technologies, customer service strategies, and other industry developments. By staying informed, businesses can ensure that their operations are running at peak efficiency and profitability.

Operations in retail are essential for businesses to succeed. By creating a plan, training team members, monitoring performance, and staying informed on industry trends, businesses can ensure that their operations are running smoothly and efficiently. With the right strategies in place, businesses can maximize their profitability and ensure long-term success.

TWENTY-THREE

Operations in Hospitality

Operations in the hospitality industry are essential for providing guests with a positive experience. From the moment a guest arrives at a hotel, restaurant, or other hospitality establishment, operations are in motion to ensure that their stay is comfortable and enjoyable. From the front desk staff to the housekeeping staff, each team member plays an important role in providing a seamless experience for the guest.

The hospitality industry is highly competitive, and operations must be managed efficiently to ensure that guests receive the best possible service. To achieve this, hospitality operations must be well-organized and managed with an eye towards efficiency. This includes ensuring that staff are properly trained and equipped to handle any situation that may arise. Additionally, it is important to have a system in place to track and monitor guest feedback, so that any issues can be addressed quickly and effectively.

In order to ensure that operations are running smoothly, it is important to have a clear understanding of the goals and objectives of the hospitality establishment. This includes understanding the target market, the services offered, and the desired customer experience. Once these goals are established, it is important to develop a plan to ensure that operations are meeting these goals. This plan should include a detailed timeline, budget, and staffing requirements.

Finally, it is important to have a system in place to measure the success of operations. This includes tracking customer feedback, analyzing operational data, and monitoring performance metrics. By doing so, hospitality establishments can ensure that operations are running smoothly and that guests are receiving the best possible service.

Operations in the hospitality industry are essential for providing guests with a positive experience. From the moment a guest arrives at a hotel, restaurant, or other hospitality establishment, operations are in motion to ensure that their stay is comfortable and enjoyable. From the front desk staff to the housekeeping staff, each team member plays an important role in providing a seamless experience for the guest. To ensure that operations are running smoothly, it is essential to have a clear understanding of the guest's journey and to have systems and procedures in place to manage the different stages of that journey. This includes managing reservations and check-in, providing room service and housekeeping, managing food and beverage service, and handling guest complaints and feedback. It also involves having effective inventory management systems to ensure that the necessary supplies and equipment are available at all times, and that they are being used in an efficient and cost-effective manner. Additionally, technology can play an important role in the operations of the hospitality industry, such as through the use of property management systems, mobile check-in and check-out, and guest feedback systems, which can help to improve the overall guest experience and increase operational efficiency.

TWENTY-FOUR

OPERATIONS IN CONSTRUCTION

Operations in construction are a critical component of any successful business. From the planning and design stages to the actual construction and completion of a project, operations play a vital role in ensuring that the project is completed on time and within budget.

The first step in any construction project is the planning and design phase. This is where the project is laid out and the scope of the project is determined. During this phase, the project manager must consider the budget, timeline, and any potential risks associated with the project. Once the project is planned and designed, the construction phase can begin.

During the construction phase, the project manager must ensure that the project is completed on time and within budget. This requires careful management of resources, including labor, materials, and equipment. The project manager must also ensure that the project is completed safely and in compliance with all applicable regulations.

Once the construction phase is complete, the project manager must ensure that the project is properly inspected and tested. This is to ensure that the project meets all applicable standards and regulations. The project manager must also ensure that the project is properly documented and that all necessary paperwork is completed.

Finally, the project manager must ensure that the project is properly maintained and that any necessary repairs or upgrades are completed. This is to ensure that the project remains in good condition and that it continues to provide value to the business.

Operations in construction are a complex and challenging endeavor. However, with careful planning, management, and execution, a successful construction project can be completed on time and within budget. By understanding the various stages of the construction process and managing the resources and risks associated with the project, a project manager can ensure that the project is completed successfully and provides value to the business.

TWENTY-FIVE

Operations in Government and Non-Profit Organizations

Government and non-profit organizations have a wide range of operations, from providing essential services to the public to managing large-scale projects. These operations are often complex and require a great deal of coordination and collaboration between different departments and stakeholders.

The operations of government and non-profit organizations are often subject to a variety of regulations and laws. This means that operations must be conducted in a way that is compliant with these regulations and laws. Additionally, these organizations must be mindful of their budgets and resources, as they are often limited.

The operations of government and non-profit organizations must also be conducted in a way that is transparent and accountable to the public. This means that operations must be conducted in a way that is open and honest, and that the public is kept informed of the progress and results of operations.

The operations of government and non-profit organizations must also be conducted in a way that is efficient and effective. This means that operations must be conducted in a way that maximizes the use of resources and minimizes waste. Additionally, operations must be conducted in a way that is responsive to the needs of the public.

Finally, the operations of government and non-profit organizations must be conducted in a way that is ethical and responsible. This means that operations must be conducted in a way that is in line with the values and mission of the organization, and that is respectful of the rights and interests of all stakeholders.

In conclusion, the operations of government and non-profit organizations are complex and require a great deal of coordination and collaboration. These operations must be conducted in a way that is compliant with regulations and laws, mindful of budgets and resources, transparent and accountable to the public, efficient and effective, and responsive to the needs of the community they serve. Effective operations management in government and non-profit organizations involves developing clear goals and objectives, creating a strategic plan and budget, and implementing processes and procedures to achieve those goals. It also involves utilizing data and metrics to track performance and make informed decisions, and fostering a culture of continuous improvement. Additionally, effective communication and collaboration among staff, stakeholders, and the community is crucial to ensure that the organization is meeting the needs of the community in an effective and efficient manner. With the right approach and mindset, government and non-profit organizations can effectively manage their operations and make a positive impact on the communities they serve.

Other Books Of The Author

1. The Moments When I Met God
2. Kashiyile Theertha Pathangal
3. GURU GYAN VANI
4. Abhiprerak Gita
5. ASSI SE JAIN GHAT TAK
6. Hopelessness of Arjuna
7. The Soul and It's True Nature
8. Sense of Action (Karma)
9. Action through Wisdom
10. Action through Wisdom
11. THEORY AND PRACTICAL OF EVERY ACTION
12. LOGICAL UNDERSTANDING OF THE SUPREME
13. THE IMPERISHABLE SUPREME
14. Yatra Nishadraj se Hanuman Ghat Tak
15. Yatra Karnatak Ghat se Raja Ghat Tak
16. Yatra Pandey Ghat se Prayagraj Ghat Tak
17. Yatra Ranjendra Prasad Ghat se Dattatreya Ghat Tak
18. YaatraSindhiya Ghat se Gwaliar Ghat Tak
19. Yatra Mangala Gauri Ghat se Hanuman Gadhi Ghat Tak
20. Yatra Gaay Ghat Se Nishad Ghat Tak
21. MAA GANGA, GHATEN EVM UTSAV
22. Ganga Arti Dev Deepavali evam Any Utsav
23. Potentials of Digitalized India
24. VEDIC CONSCIOUSNESS
25. A Brief Introduction to Vedic Science
26. Kashi ke Barah Jyotirling
27. IMPACT OF MOTIVATION
28. Let's have a Milky Way Journey
29. Color Therapy in a Nutshell

30. Rigveda in a Nutshell
31. Yajurveda in a Nutshell
32. Samveda in a Nutshell
33. Atharva Veda in a Nutshell
34. Ayushman Bhava - Ayurveda
35. Srimad Bhagavad Gita and Upanishad Connection
36. Srimad Bhagavad Gita - an attempt to summarize each chapter.
37. Facts and Impact of Nakshatra
38. Astro Gems - NAVARATNA
39. Ekadashi - A Concise Overview
40. A Concise View of Hanuman Chalisa
41. Inspirational Gita
42. Nakshatraranyam
43. Summary of 18 Mahapuranas
44. Synopsis of 18 Upa Puranas
45. Rigvediya Upanishads
46. Shukla Yajurvediya Upanishads
47. Krishna Yajurvediya Upanishads
48. Samavediya Upanishads
49. Atharvavediya Upanishads
50. The Seven Great Sages
51. From Rocket Scientist to President Dr. APJ Abdul Kalam
52. The Visionary's Voice - Quotes of Dr. APJ Abdul Kalam
53. The Wisdom of Swami Vivekananda: Insights and Inspiration from a Legendary Spiritual Teacher
54. Ayurvedic Remedies from the Garden
55. Sages and Seers
56. Rising Strong – Motivational Stories of Women
57. Beyond Flames -Mystery stories of Funeral Ghat Manikarnika
58. The Origins of Tulsi: A Look at the Mythological Roots of the Plant"

59. The Holistic Cow: A Look at the Physical, Spiritual, and Cultural Importance of Cows in India
60. Arts of Healing
61. Exploring the Divine
62. Understanding Five Elements
63. The Etymology of Ram
64. Symbols of India
65. Voice of Change (About Speeches of Great Men)
66. She Speaks (About Speeches of Great Women)
67. Patriotism on Celluloid – Brief About Patriotic Films
68. The Music of Motivation: A Brief Guide to Inspirational Film Songs
69. **Unlocking the Secrets of the Dashopanishads**
70. A Cultural Mosaic
71. Ancient Traditions, Modern Minds
72. Ecos of Ancient Wisdom
73. Beneath the Surface
74. From Temples to Ashrams
75. Sages of the Subcontinent
76. The Art of Healling (Ayurveda, Yoga & Naturopathy)
77. Indian Kitchen
78. The Festivals of India
79. The Indian Epics Retold
80. The Power of Mantras
81. The Indian River Ganges
82. The Indian Architecture
83. Rites of Passage
84. The Indian Silk Road
85. The Indian Literature
86. The Indian Villages
87. The Indian Folks & Crafts
88. The Way of Buddha
89. The Ramayan of Tulsidas

90. Astrological Remedies
91. The Secret Power of Motivation
92. Secret of Developing your Inner Strength
93. The Secret Path to Motivation
94. The Art and Secret of Positive Thinking
95. The Secrets of Practicing Ethical Living
96. Indian Art and Painting
97. The Indian Herbalism
98. Bharatanatyam to Kathak
99. Exploring India's Astrological Remedies
100. The Indian Festival of Flowers
101. Indian Handicrafts
102. The Splashes of Joy – India's Colour Festival
103. The Indian Science of Astrology
104. The Indian Mythology
105. Path to Enlightenment
106. The Indian Spirituality for Children
107. Aromas of India
108. The Secrets of Healthy Relationships
109. Ancestral Ties
110. The Indian Street Food
111. Discovering America
112. The Indian Textile
113. Listening to Motivational Speeches
114. Taste of India
115. A Cultural Journey through Indian Nuptials
116. Motivational Quote for Change
117. Secret Strategies for Making Money
118. Secrets to Cultivate a Positive Mindset
119. A Tapestry of Cultures: Exploring India from Kashmir to Kanyakumari
120. Achieving Your Dreams with Resilience: Secret Strategies for Overcoming Obstacles

121. Innovative Startups - 25 Startup Ideas to Spark Your Business Creativity
122. Export Management: Strategies for Global Success
123. Exporting from India - A Step by Step Guide
124. Finance Fundamentals: Mastering Financial Management for Business Success
125. Global Growth Strategies for International Business Development
126. Marketing Mastery: Unlocking the Secrets of Modern Marketing
127. Operations Mastery: Managing the Flow of Value in Business
128. Strategic Business Management: Navigating the Modern Business Landscape
129. Human Resource Management Strategies for Building and Managing a High Performance Team
130. The Indian Landscapes And Nature: An Exploration Of India's Natural Beauty And Diversity

Contact

DR. JAGADEESH PILLAI

MBA & PhD in Vedic Science

Four Times Guinness World Record Holder

Winner of Mahatma Gandhi Vishwa Shanti Puraskar and Global Peace Ambassador

Gemology, Astro & Vastu Consultant - Spiritual Counselor

Consultant for designing World Record Ideas

Efficient Tarot Card Reader

9839093003

myrichindia@gmail.com

drjagadeeshpillai@facebook

drjagadeeshpillai@instagram
jagadeeshpillai@youtube

www. JAGADEESHPILLAI.com

|| LOKAHA SAMASTHAHA SUKHINO BHAVANTU ||

9 798889 590453

Printed by Libri Plureos GmbH in Hamburg,
Germany